LEVEL 1

SCHOLASTIC

Adapted by: Lynda Edwards
Based on the book by Lois Duncan
Screenplay by Jeff Lowell and Bob Schooley & Mark McCorkle

Publisher: Jacquie Bloese

Editor: Fiona Davis

Designer: Dawn Wilson

Cover layout: Dawn Wilson

Picture research: Pupak Navabpour

Photo credits:
Pages 34 & 35: Aardman, Cinetext, Element Films/Allstar; C Furlong/Getty Images; RIA Novosti/Alamy.
Pages 36 & 37: The Guide Dogs for the Blind Association; M Abrahams/Alamy; A Barclay/Rex.

© 2010 DW Studios LLC. All Rights Reserved.

Published by Scholastic Ltd. 2010

No part of this publication may be reproduced in whole or in part, or stored in a retrieval system, or transmitted in any form or by any means, electronic, mechanical, photocopying, recording or otherwise, without written permission of the publisher. For information regarding permission write to:

Mary Glasgow Magazines (Scholastic Ltd.)
Euston House
24 Eversholt Street
London NW1 IDB

All rights reserved

Printed in Malaysia

Reprinted in 2010, 2011, 2014, 2015, 2016, 2017 and 2018

Contents	Page
Hotel for Dogs	4–31
People and Places	4
Chapter 1: Andi's family	6
Chapter 2: The old hotel	10
Chapter 3: Friday's new friends	15
Chapter 4: The Hotel for Dogs	18
Chapter 5: A terrible night	22
Chapter 6: Follow the van!	25
Chapter 7: A new family	28
Epilogue	31
Fact Files	32–37
Hotel for Dogs: the film	32
Famous dogs	34
Working dogs	36
Self-Study Activities	38–40
New Words	inside back cover

PEOPLE AND PLACES

HOTEL FOR DOGS

ANDI is sixteen years old. She lives with her brother, Bruce,  and their dog, Friday. Andi and Bruce's parents died and now they live with Carl and Lois.

BRUCE is eleven. He's very good at inventing things. He  and Andi are sometimes in trouble. And it's usually because of Friday …

FRIDAY loves Andi and Bruce very much, and they love  him. Friday is always hungry. He's a very clever dog. He's often in trouble but people are never angry with Friday!

LENNY, GEORGIA AND THEIR FRIENDS

are all looking for a home and a family.

CARL AND LOIS want to be music stars … but they're not very good. They don't like children or dogs, and they don't know about Friday …

BERNIE finds new families for children. He's a good, kind man and he cares a lot about Andi and Bruce.

DAVE loves dogs. He works in the pet shop. He likes Andi and wants to know her better.

HEATHER also works in the pet shop.

PLACES

THE HOTEL People stayed in this beautiful hotel a long time ago. Now it's dark and empty.

THE POUND The Animal Control men look for dogs on the streets and bring them to the pound. The men at this pound don't care about the dogs. Sometimes the owners don't come for their dogs and then the men kill them.

PRIMARY PAWS This is the pet shop. Dave and Heather work here.

CHAPTER 1
Andi's family

Hi, I'm Friday! And I'm a dog. I'm waiting for my owners, Andi and Bruce. Hmm ... this is boring and I'm hungry. Hey, I smell sausages! Who's eating sausages? I'm going to follow that smell. Maybe today is my lucky day ...

Andi walked into the shop. There were lots of people inside. People took things there to sell. Andi had a box with a picture of a mobile phone on it. She looked at the picture and smiled. There wasn't a phone inside the box. There were just some stones!

Andi smiled at the shop owner. She had big, beautiful eyes and dark hair.

'Do you buy phones? This is new,' she said.

The shop owner looked at her. 'How old are you?'

'Eighteen,' Andi said.

The shop owner said nothing. He didn't believe her.
'Oh, OK … I'm sixteen.'
'No, thanks,' he said.

Andi walked out sadly. Another man from the shop followed her. 'Wait!' he said. He looked at the box. It was a good phone. 'Here's twenty dollars.' He gave her the money. Andi gave him the box and ran.

She found Bruce at the corner of the street.

'Did you sell it?' he asked.

'Yes – for twenty dollars!' Andi smiled.

'Twenty dollars for some stones in a box!' Bruce was happy.

'And now we've got money for Friday's food!' Andi said.

Andi and Bruce looked for Friday. They found him in the street.

'Friday!' called Bruce happily. 'Where were you?' He gave Friday a big hug. 'Here, boy,' he said. 'Burgers!'

Friday ate the burgers very quickly.

Andi laughed. 'He's always hungry!'

Suddenly she looked up. 'Oh no!' she said quietly. There was a policeman in front of them. The man from the shop was with him. He looked very angry.

'I can't believe it! Not again!' Bernie drove Andi and Bruce from the police station to Carl and Lois's flat. 'Do this again and you leave Carl and Lois!'

Andi laughed. 'Great!'

'No,' said Bernie, 'it's not great. I can't keep you together again. That's five families in three years.'

Andi and Bruce were quiet. They were brother and sister. They wanted to stay together. But they wanted a new home. They wanted a family for Friday too.

Andi and Bruce stopped outside the door of the flat. The music was terrible. Carl and Lois were in a band. Carl played guitar and Lois was the singer. But she didn't sing – she shouted to the music. Cats were better singers!

Andi looked at Bruce and pushed open the door.

'You're late!' shouted Lois. Her hair was very yellow and her eyes were very black. She wanted to be a pop star and she tried to look young. Carl wanted to be a star too. He had long, dirty hair and a stupid smile.

Lois started to shout to the music again. Andi and Bruce ran to the bedroom and closed the door.

'Wow!' said Bruce. 'They're worse than before. Is that possible?'

There was a little bark. Friday was outside the window. During the day, the little dog lived outside. At night, he stayed in the bedroom.

Tonight they were all tired. Bruce went to sleep quickly. Friday was in his arms. Andi watched them. The little dog looked at her. There was a lot of love in his eyes. Next to Bruce's bed, there was a photograph of their mum and dad. Andi looked at the photograph. She was very sad. She wanted to keep her little family together – her, Bruce and Friday. But it was so difficult.

'What are we going to do?' she asked quietly in the dark.

CHAPTER 2
The old hotel

It's breakfast time and I can smell ... yes ... sausages! So ... where are they? Let's try the kitchen. Yes, I see them. That person with the yellow hair can't sing but she can cook good sausages! How can I get there? OK ... jump on the table. Careful, Friday! I don't want her to see me. I can go behind this bag. Hmm ... now what am I going to do?

'Good morning!' Andi called loudly to Lois.

Lois turned round quickly. 'You're early!' she said, surprised. Behind her, Friday had two large sausages in his mouth.

Lois turned back again. Quickly Bruce took Friday in his arms and ran into the bedroom. Andi ran after them and closed the bedroom door.

'Don't go in the kitchen again!' Bruce put Friday outside the window. 'One day Lois is going to see you!'

Carl and Lois's flat was on the fifth floor. It was a long way down to the street but Friday was lucky. He sat in a box. The box went down to the street. It was one of Bruce's inventions.

It was early but there were a lot of people in the street. Friday looked round.

> That was a great breakfast! Now where can I go today? Maybe the park? Maybe I can meet some new friends. Let's go down here and across the road. Oops! Sorry, I didn't see your foot. Wow! You've got very big feet. Oh no! It's the Animal Control man. Now I'm in BIG trouble!

'Do you know this dog?' Andi and Bruce were in the pet shop. 'His name's Friday. We can't find him.'

Dave looked carefully at the picture of the little white dog.

'Friday! That's a funny name!' He smiled at Andi. Andi smiled back.

Bruce looked at Andi and then at Dave. 'Can we go now?' he asked.

'I'm sorry,' said Dave. 'Maybe he's in the pound.'

There were a lot of dogs in the pound. Some were small and some were big. But they were all sad and frightened.

The Animal Control man had a hard face and his eyes were cold. 'Do you want your dog?' he asked. 'Bring your parents.'

Andi took all her money from her bag and put it on the table. 'There,' she said.

The man smiled. It wasn't a nice smile. 'OK. You can have your dog.'

Andi and Bruce walked home with Friday through the dark streets. Andi looked at her brother.

'We can't leave Friday on his own,' she said. 'He needs a good home with a good family.'

Bruce didn't understand. 'He's got a home and he's got a family,' he said. 'That's us!' He was angry. Friday was his best friend.

It was late and there weren't many people in the street. They were outside an old, empty hotel. Suddenly Friday's ears went up. He heard something. The little dog ran through an open door into the dark hotel.

'Friday! Come back!' shouted Andi. She and Bruce followed him into the hotel. Then they stopped.

They were in a different world. The hotel was old and dirty, but it was very big. It had lovely windows and a fantastic staircase. Andi looked round. Once this was a beautiful building with a lot of expensive things. She saw again the tables and chairs and the pretty lights. She saw rich people in their lovely clothes. The people walked and talked and danced in this big room. But now the big room was dark and empty. There were boxes and old things everywhere. No one loved this place. No one danced here now.

Suddenly Bruce pulled her arm. 'Listen!' He was

frightened. 'Did you hear that? Someone's here.'

They both looked towards the sound. Who was it? They were ready to run.

'Look!' said Bruce quietly.

A very big dog was at the bottom of the stairs. But he wasn't alone. There was another dog too. This one was very small and she sat between his legs. In their eyes was a question: What are you doing here?

CHAPTER 3
Friday's new friends

 Wow! This hotel is a really nice place to live. It's better than the street! Hi, guys! Can I be in your club? Can I? Please?

The small dog ran off up the stairs. Friday and the big dog followed. They ran into a bedroom. Andi and Bruce followed them. All three dogs jumped onto the big bed. Then they closed their eyes and went to sleep.

'They look so happy!' smiled Andi.

'Maybe we can leave Friday with them tonight,' said Bruce. 'I think he's got some new friends. We can call the big one Lenny, and the little one is Georgia.'

Andi thought for a moment.

'OK, just one night,' she said and closed the bedroom blind. 'Goodnight, guys!'

Early the next morning, there was a loud howling. It was very loud and it didn't stop. Andi looked at Bruce. They ran to the hotel. They didn't want the Animal Control men to hear it too.

In the bedroom Lenny sat by the window. His big mouth was open and he howled and howled. It was a terrible sound! Friday and Georgia were under the bed.

'It's the blind!' shouted Andi. She opened the blind quickly and Lenny stopped. He looked at the sky. He was happy now.

Andi went to the pet shop to buy more dog food. Dave was surprised. 'That's a lot of food for one little dog!'

Andi smiled. 'This is for three dogs. My mum and dad love dogs. We give a home to dogs from the street.' She didn't want to tell him about Carl and Lois.

'Great!' Dave smiled back. 'Come with me.'

There were three dogs in the back room. 'That's Cooper. He eats everything! This is Shep. She runs round everyone! And that's Romeo. He's always frightened. They all need a home too. Can you take them?'

Andi opened her mouth. 'But ...'

Dave looked at Andi. He had very nice brown eyes, she thought. 'I can pay for the dog food,' he said. 'I don't want to send them to the pound. Please?'

At the hotel, Bruce found a big red book on the table. He opened it. It was the hotel book. This book had lots of people's names in it. Bruce found a pen and carefully wrote *Friday* in the book. He stopped and smiled.

Then he looked up and saw Andi with Dave.

'What's wrong?' he asked. Were they in trouble?

'I want to help,' smiled Dave. 'And it's OK. I'm not going to tell anyone.'

'I can help too!' A pretty girl came through the door. Heather also worked in the pet shop. 'I followed your van, Dave. Ugh! What's this?' She looked at her shoe. There was dog poo all over the floor. She smiled. 'I can clean up!'

Andi looked at her brother. It wasn't only their problem now. They weren't alone. 'OK,' laughed Andi. 'Now there's four of us – and six of them!'

CHAPTER 4
The Hotel for Dogs

Andi and Bruce and their new friends cleaned the hotel. They gave food to the dogs and they took them all for walks. At the end of the day they sat on the floor of the hotel. They were very tired, but the dogs weren't.

'We can't do this!' said Andi. 'They still want to play. And there's poo everywhere. We clean it up and they poo again!'

'They're dogs!' laughed Dave.

Bruce went to the table and took some paper. There was a light in his eyes. 'I've got the answer!' he said.

He sat down and drew a picture. Then he started to make a machine. He worked quickly. Soon it was ready.

'Hey, Georgia!' he called. 'Come and play!' Georgia loved running after things. He put his foot on the machine and it hit a ball across the room. Georgia ran after the ball. She loved it.

'Wow!' said Dave. 'That's fantastic! Where did you learn to do that?'

'My dad,' Bruce said. Andi hugged him. Bruce smiled and started to plan some more machines for the dogs.

WALKING MACHINE
There is a bone on the machine. The dogs walk after it. Then they're tired and we're not!

FOOD MACHINE
A train brings food for the dogs when we're not here!

DOG GAMES
The dogs watch a film of a road and they think they're in a car!

THE POO MACHINE
The dogs poo in a special place and the machine washes it away. A clean hotel!

The friends worked hard. Soon the different machines were ready. The hotel was clean and the dogs were happy.

Then Bruce had another good idea. 'This hotel is big,' he said. 'And there are a lot of dogs on the streets!'

The others were excited.

'Of course!' said Heather. 'We can give them a home!'

'It's the Hotel for Dogs!' cried Bruce.

Bruce listened to his radio. On the radio he could hear the Animal Control man.

Quickly he phoned Dave in his van. 'There's a dog on 6th Street,' he said. 'Be quick!'

When the Animal Control man arrived at 6th Street, Andi and Heather were there. They started to talk to him. Dave ran behind them and took the dog in his arms. When the Animal Control man looked for the dog, the dog wasn't there.

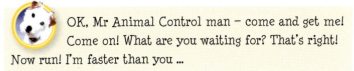

OK, Mr Animal Control man – come and get me! Come on! What are you waiting for? That's right! Now run! I'm faster than you ...

The Animal Control man ran after Friday. Andi, Bruce and the others opened the back of his van. All the dogs ran out. The van was empty. The streets were empty. And now the pound was empty too! All the dogs were in the hotel.

Life was busy for Andi and Bruce now. They didn't have time to think about their problems with Carl and Lois. They were surprised when Bernie wanted to talk to them.

'I've got something good to tell you,' he smiled. 'I have a lovely family for you. You can leave Carl and Lois!'

Andi looked at Bruce. This was fantastic. 'That's great, Bernie! Thank you very much!' She hugged him.

Bernie laughed. 'That's OK. You're going to love these people. And it's not very far away. Only three hours.'

'What?' Andi stopped smiling. Three hours! What about the hotel, the dogs and their friends?

'Sorry, Bernie,' said Bruce slowly. 'We've got friends here now. We don't want to move.'

'I don't understand,' said Bernie. 'You hate Carl and Lois!'

Andi and Bruce walked back to the hotel. They wanted to leave Carl and Lois but the hotel was their family now.

CHAPTER 5
A terrible night

Andi was excited. Dave wanted her to go to a party with him. She found a dress in the hotel. She looked beautiful.

It was a good party. Andi met a lot of Dave's friends. She liked Dave. He was kind and he was good-looking. But he still didn't know about her family.

Then something terrible happened.

'Hi, Andi!' A boy smiled at her. 'You live near me. You live with Carl and Lois!'

'No, I don't!' she said loudly.

Dave looked at her. What was the problem? Why was Andi's face so white?

'It isn't true.' Andi turned quickly. But someone was behind her with some drinks. She didn't see him. The drinks went on the floor and over her lovely dress.

Andi cried and ran out of the room. Life is never going to be good for me, she thought.

Bruce had a big problem too. Lois found some of her things in Bruce's bag. He used a lot of things from the flat for his machines. She was very angry.

'Sit there!' she shouted. 'I'm calling the police!'

 Oh dear. We've got a problem here. Where's the food? We're all here. We're waiting. Oh no! The machine isn't working! Bruce, where are you?

The dogs were hungry but there was no food and no Bruce. They ran into the kitchen and opened all the boxes. They left things all over the floor.

Then Georgia remembered something. There was a bone on the walking machine! She was little but she was a good jumper. She soon got the bone. But now she had a problem. All the dogs in the hotel wanted it too. They ran after her. They ran through all the bedrooms. They pushed over machines. But Georgia still had the bone.

Bruce could hear the loud barking and howling. It was the dogs! Lois was on the phone to the police. Quickly and quietly he left the flat and ran to the hotel.

There was food everywhere and his beautiful machines were on the floor. The dogs were all over the hotel. They were angry and hungry.

'What happened?' Andi came through the door. She looked round. 'I can't believe it.' The party was bad but this was worse! Then they heard the police car. 'Quick, Bruce! Find the dogs! Get them in one room!' she cried.

Andi, Bruce and the dogs sat very quietly in one of the bedrooms. Andi turned off the lights. Andi turned off all the lights.

'Who's there?' shouted a policeman.

Good dogs, thought Bruce. Just one more minute. Then he looked at the window. The blind was closed. Oh no! He looked at Lenny. The big dog opened his mouth and started to howl! Was this the end of the Hotel for Dogs?

CHAPTER 6
Follow the van!

Oh no! Not again! Put me down! No, don't put me in this horrible van! I want to be with Andi and Bruce. Where are they going? Why are they with those men? Don't cry, Andi. Somebody help me!

'We're in big trouble this time.' Andi looked at Bernie. 'We're very sorry. Please help us.'

'There's nothing I can do this time, Andi.' Bernie was sad. He loved Andi and Bruce but it was too late. Carl and Lois were very angry. They didn't want them in the flat. No one wanted them. 'You're going to different homes.'

'No!' cried Andi. 'Bruce needs me.'

Bruce hugged her. 'It's OK,' he said. 'We tried to save the dogs. That's the important thing. Remember that.'

Come on, everyone! We can't just sit here and do nothing. Look, that door's open. I'm going to get out and find help. See you later, boys! Who can help me now? I know ... Dave! Which way to the pet shop?

Andi was in a home for girls. She was very sad. But then she heard a bark. She went to the window. A boy and a dog were outside. Was it …? Yes, it was Dave and Friday!

'We've got a plan!' Dave told her. 'We're going to find the dogs. Then we're going to take them to a pound in a different part of the city. They don't kill them there. We can still save them.'

'Fantastic!' cried Andi. 'Let's find Bruce!'

Bernie went into the hotel. He looked around the hotel and saw Bruce's inventions. Then he found the red hotel book. He opened it and started reading.

Lenny and Georgia: the first dogs in our new family.
Madison, 3rd August: Madison was in a back garden. Her family moved away and left her.

Bernie was very quiet. Now he understood.

Dave stopped his van outside the pound. The back door was open and there were a lot of sausages inside. That was part of the plan.

'Fire!' shouted Heather. She ran to the door of the pound. 'Come quickly!'

When the Animal Control man came out, Andi, Bruce

and Friday went in. They quickly opened all the doors and the dogs ran out happily.

The van waited outside. Andi and Bruce jumped in. The dogs smelled the sausages.

'Come on,' cried Bruce. 'This way! Follow the van!' The van drove away. The dogs ran after the sausages.

'Yes!' shouted Dave. 'They're coming!' He drove through the city. The dogs came too. People watched and laughed. They took photos as the dogs ran through the busy city streets. It was fantastic! They were almost there. They were almost at the other pound.

Suddenly Friday turned right. He went down a different street. The other dogs followed him.

'Where's he going?' shouted Andi.
'Oh no!' said Bruce. 'He's going back to the hotel.'

CHAPTER 7
A new family

The dogs ran through the streets to the hotel and Dave's van followed them. The police and the Animal Control men followed Dave and the dogs. A lot of people came too. Soon everyone was in the hotel.

The Animal Control man felt important. 'It's OK, everyone!' he said loudly. 'We're going to take all these dirty, old dogs to the pound.'

Andi and Bruce pushed through the crowd. 'Wait!' shouted Andi. She was angry. 'You can't take them. They're ours.'

'They're our family!' cried Bruce.

The Animal Control man laughed. 'Take these children out of here!' he said to a policeman.

'Stop!' Suddenly everyone was quiet. There was a man at the top of the staircase. It was Bernie. He had the red hotel book in his hand.

'Listen to me before you kill these dogs,' he said quietly. 'I know these two kids. They were wrong but they tried to help. They saved these dogs and they made their own family.'

The Animal Control man laughed again. 'Yeah – a family of dirty, old street dogs!'

Bernie looked at him coldly. The man was quiet. Bernie opened the red book. 'Madison!' he called. No one moved. It was very quiet in the hotel.

'Madison!' he called again. A little dog came to the top of the stairs. She sat down by Bernie and looked at all the people.

Bernie smiled at her. He read from the book. *'Madison, 3rd August: Madison was in a back garden. Her family moved away and left her.'*

He called again. 'Viola and Sebastian!' Two small brown dogs came and sat on the stairs. *'Viola and Sebastian were by a busy road. Viola was hurt but her brother didn't leave her.'*

Bernie slowly called all the dogs and they came and sat on the stairs. 'These dogs aren't dirty street dogs,' he told the people in the hotel. 'Andi and Bruce saved them. This hotel is a home and a family for these dogs. Don't take it away.'

The policeman looked at Bernie and he looked at Andi and Bruce. He looked at all the people. And the people looked at him.

'OK!' said the policeman. 'They can stay!'

Everyone cheered.

Andi and Bruce jumped up and down. 'I can't believe it!' cried Andi. 'Thank you, Bernie!'

Bernie smiled. Then he saw his wife. She pushed through the people. 'I have another surprise. I found a new family for you.' he said.

'For us? For both of us?' asked Bruce.

'Yes,' said Bernie. 'This family likes children *and* dogs! Would you like to live with us?' He put his arm round his wife.

'Yes!' Bruce and Andi shouted. Now they had everything – a family, Friday and the Hotel for Dogs!

EPILOGUE

Hi, everyone! This is my new hotel – the Hotel for Dogs! It's fantastic. We've got everything for you. There is a bone in every room! Don't forget to try the games room – it's great fun. Do you want to look beautiful? We've got a special wash room. Do your owners want a new dog? They can find one here too. And I must tell you about the restaurant. The food is great. We've got burgers and sausages, of course! Mmm. And when you're eating, you can listen to our band. Do you know them? It's Carl and Lois! My friend, Lenny, likes to sing with them. Listen! Aaouwwh!

FACT FILE

HOTEL FOR DOGS
THE FILM

The film *Hotel for Dogs* is great fun! It was great fun to make too – for the actors and, of course, the dogs!

Working with dogs!

Everyone loved the dogs! But it wasn't always easy. Sometimes there were more than 120 dogs in one scene!

Jake T. Austin is Bruce. 'Usually on a film everyone is really quiet. On this film it wasn't quiet at all,' he remembers. 'Sometimes there were ten or twelve dog trainers. They all said 'Sit!' or 'Stay!' to their dogs at the same time!'

Sometimes the dogs were very good and did things right. But not always. 'In the hotel I walk up the staircase with Friday and Georgia. They filmed that seventeen times. The dogs were always in the wrong place!' says Jake.

Kyla Pratt (Heather) loved the dogs. 'I prefer to work with crazy dogs than crazy actors!' she laughs.

The real stars

The dog actors were the real stars of the film. There were big and small dogs and dogs of different colours. For some of the dogs, they had two or three dog actors.

There were three different dog actors for Friday! One was Friday from the front. One was Friday from the back. And one was Friday when he ran!

THE ACTORS

Lisa Kudrow plays Lois in the film. Do you remember her? She was Phoebe in *Friends*. 'In Hotel for Dogs I sing very badly,' says Lisa. 'It's easier than singing well!'

Emma Roberts started to act when she was nine. She is the niece of actor, Julia Roberts. 'I loved working on *Hotel for Dogs*,' she says. 'The dogs were great!'

Would you like to watch *Hotel for Dogs*? Why / Why not?

The machines

Bruce invents a lot of crazy and clever machines in the film. There were special designers to make the machines for the dogs. The designers had a great time. The dogs loved the throwing machine! Some of the machines were difficult to design. But in the film they all look very easy!

Did you know?

Hotel for Dogs is a very popular book. Lois Duncan wrote the book in 1971. Lois says, 'I was very happy to see the film. Dogs still have a lot of problems today. People can learn about these from the film.'

What do these words mean? You can use a dictionary.
act / actor   scene   crazy   real   design / designer   niece   popular

FACT FILE

FAMOUS DOGS

Everyone loves dogs. We love watching them in films and reading about them in books. Here are some dogs that are famous all over the world. Do you know why they are famous?

Greyfriars Bobby

Bobby was a real dog. He lived in the 1850s in Edinburgh, in Scotland. His story is very sad. Bobby's owner was John Gray and for two years they went everywhere together. In 1858 Gray died. For the next fourteen years Bobby sat on his grave. He only left for his food or when it got very cold in the winter. Today there is a statue of the little dog near John Gray's grave.

Laika

A lot of people know about this dog, but they don't know her name. In 1957 Laika went 2,000 miles into space. Russian scientists found Laika in the streets in Moscow. She didn't have a home. They trained her to travel into space. Sadly, Laika died. But we learned a lot about space travel because of this dog.

Lassie

Lassie is probably the most famous dog in film. There are more than ten films and many TV series about her. Lassie is beautiful and clever. She always helps her owners when they're in trouble. The first Lassie film was in 1943 but they are still making Lassie films today. Of course, it's not the same dog actor! A dog called Pal played Lassie in the first film. Many dogs from Pal's family are in later films.

Gromit

Gromit is one of the world's funniest dogs. Gromit can't talk but he's very clever. He's good at inventing machines. He does a lot of exciting things with his owner, Wallace. Gromit is one of the best-loved stars in the UK today.

Can you think of a famous dog in your country? Why is it famous?

What do these words mean? You can use a dictionary.
real   grave   statue   space   scientist   travel (n/v)   TV series

FACT FILE

WORKING DOGS

Some people say: 'A dog is a man's best friend'. But dogs are not just fantastic pets. They help us too. There are lots of different working dogs.

Guide dogs

The first guide dogs
When soldiers came home after the First World War (1914–18), many of them were blind. In Germany they started to train dogs to help the soldiers. The dogs were the soldiers' eyes.

Guide dogs today A young guide dog lives with a family for a year. These people teach them to do easy things like sitting, walking and waiting. They also teach them to be good with people and other dogs. Then the dogs go to a special school. It takes a long time and costs a lot of money.

Now there are dogs for deaf people too. At home they listen for the sound of the phone or when someone is at the door. They can keep their owners out of danger too. They can hear if something is wrong.

Did you know?
When guide dogs are out with their owner, they are working. It's not a good idea to talk to a guide dog in the street, or give it food.

> Do you ever see working dogs? Where do you see them?

Police dogs

A job in the police

Dogs have very good noses! They can smell many different things. They can smell many things that we can't. Dogs can find things like guns in people's bags. They also find things in cars and vans. Sometimes they even find people. The dogs like this work – for them it is a game.

Police also use dogs to stop criminals. They are very strong and sometimes jump at people with guns.

> **What do these words mean? You can use a dictionary.**
> soldier   blind   deaf   danger   smell   guns   criminals

Good friends

Police dogs are working dogs. They don't live with their owner in their home. They live outside because they are not pets. When they are old and stop work, sometimes their owner keeps them. Then they are pets.

SELF-STUDY ACTIVITIES

CHAPTERS 1-2

Before you read

1 Read 'People and places' on pages 4–5. Answer these questions.
   a) Who wants to be in a band?
   b) Who is always hungry?
   c) Who works in a pet shop?
   d) Who invents things?
   e) Who finds new families for children?
   f) Who is Bruce's sister?
   g) Where do street dogs go?

2 Match these words with the sentences.
   a bark   a box   sausages   stairs   stones
   a) Dogs make this sound.
   b) Some people eat these for breakfast.
   c) You can put things in this.
   d) You can find these by the sea.
   e) You go up these in a house.

After you read

3 Complete the sentences with these words.
   jumps   hugs   outside   smell
   a) Friday can … sausages and follows the man in the street.
   b) Bruce … Friday when he finds him in the street.
   c) The little dog … on the table to find the sausages.
   d) Friday hears a sound when they are … the hotel.

4 Answer the questions.
   a) Why do Andi and Bruce need some money?
   b) Who drives Andi and Bruce home from the police station?
   c) Why does Friday stay outside during the day?
   d) Who finds Friday in the street and where does he take him?
   e) Why do the children go into the old hotel?

5 What do you think?
   a) Andi and Bruce are sometimes in trouble, but are they bad?
   b) Do Andi and Bruce like living with Carl and Lois? Why / Why not?

CHAPTERS 3–4

Before you read

6 Choose the right answer.
   a) Where can you find a **blind**?
      i) on the floor   ii) at the window   iii) on the wall
   b) A dog **howls** when …
      i) it's sad   ii) it's happy   iii) it's friendly
   c) If something is **horrible**, it is …
      i) nice   ii) useful   iii) frightening
   d) Dogs like to find …
      i) phones   ii) stones   iii) bones
   e) You can drive a …
      i) boat   ii) bicycle   iii) van

After you read

7 Complete the sentences with these names.
   Bruce   Dave   Friday   Georgia   Heather   Lenny
   a) … stays at the Hotel for the night.
   b) Friday's new friends are Lenny and … .
   c) … howls at the window in the morning.
   d) … gives Andi three more dogs.
   e) … follows the van to the Hotel.
   f) … invents some machines for the dogs.

8 Are the sentences true or false? Correct the false sentences.
   a) Andi tells Dave about Carl and Lois.
   b) Andi goes to the pet shop to buy more dogs.
   c) Bruce makes a machine to bring food for the dogs.
   d) Bruce makes a machine to give the dogs a hug.
   e) The teenagers decide to save the dogs from the pound.
   f) Bernie finds a new family for Andi and Bruce.
   g) Andi and Bruce leave Carl and Lois.

9 What do you think?
   a) Is the Hotel for Dogs a good idea?
   b) What are the Animal Control men going to do?

SELF-STUDY ACTIVITIES

CHAPTERS 5–7 & EPILOGUE

Before you read

10 What do you think?
   Chapter 5 is called *A terrible night*. Who is going to get in trouble in this chapter?

After you read

11 Who says these words?
   a) 'I'm calling the police.'
   b) 'Oh no! The machine isn't working!'
   c) 'There's nothing I can do.'
   d) 'We tried to save the dogs. That's the important thing.'
   e) 'We can still save them.'
   f) 'Follow the van!'
   g) 'They were wrong but they tried to help.'
   h) 'They can stay!'

12 Complete the sentences
   a) Lois was angry because …
   b) The dogs ran after Georgia because …
   c) Dave wants to take the dogs to a different pound because …
   d) The dogs follow the van because …
   e) Bernie understands about the hotel because …
   f) Andi and Bruce are happy because …

13 Which of these things *can't* dogs do at the Hotel for Dogs?
   a) eat in the restaurant
   b) listen to some music
   c) have a wash
   d) have a bone
   e) use the computer

14 What do you think?
   a) Who do you like best in the story? Why?
   b) What can people learn from this story?